The Rose That Blooms in the Night

The Rose That Blooms in the Night

Andrews McMeel Publishing
a division of Andrews McMeel Universal
1130 Walnut Street, Kansas City, Missouri 64106

www.andrewsmcmeel.com

22 23 24 25 26 VEP 10 9 8 7 6 5 4 3 2

ISBN: 978-1-5248-5363-1

Library of Congress Control Number: 2019938760

Editor: Patty Rice
Art Directors: Diane Marsh and Tiffany Meairs
Production Editor: Elizabeth A. Garcia
Production Manager: Cliff Koehler

Cover illustration by Rebecca Reitz

ATTENTION: SCHOOLS AND BUSINESSES
Andrews McMeel books are available at quantity discounts with
bulk purchase for educational, business, or sales promotional use.
For information, please e-mail the Andrews McMeel Publishing
Special Sales Department: specialsales@amuniversal.com.

ALSO BY ALLIE MICHELLE

Explorations of a Cosmic Soul

The Rose That Blooms in the Night

ALLIE MICHELLE

Andrews McMeel
PUBLISHING®

For my mother, the rose that bloomed
in the night. These poems would
not exist without you.

Find the strength it takes to be soft.

—ALLIE MICHELLE

Part 1: Dusk

Rose of the Night

Have you heard the story of the rose
That blooms in the night?
Without the Sun's presence
She grew from her own light
She did not yearn for
His warmth on her petals
For she knew she held the power
To radiate light from within
Though she had strong thorns
Her heart was always open
For those with an open heart
Can never be broken

Wings

I once knew a bird who was tamed by being convinced she was broken. They trained her to believe that if she attempted to fly free, she would experience pain. Her cage then started to feel safe. She could avoid pain within those four walls. But then something else happened. Those wings that were meant to soar lost their strength. Her life force weakened from not using her gifts, and she experienced deep sorrow. She was born a wild thing, you see. And though it was far more terrifying for her to explore the edges of this uncertain world, it was also what made her very blood sing. Her mind entrapped her within this room of doubt, but her heart knew the gate had been open the entire time. Have you allowed yourself to become caged, my love?

Oxygen of Life

love is always pressing onto your body
as the sea does to a fish,
and yet the fish is unaware of the water that surrounds it
so what are we to do about this?
they say love is the oxygen of life,
but why do I see so many people gasping for air
when all they need do is inhale?

Puzzle Pieces

I dreamed I saw each person as a walking puzzle piece. Each one whole, yet part of a greater picture. I watched as some of the pieces fit together, adding to each other's masterpiece. Then there were the ones that looked close to fitting but maybe weren't quite right. And I saw how, out of fear, they forced themselves to fit until their edges became soft and molded into an entirely different shape. What they did not realize was that the shape they had before was perfect. Now the piece originally meant for them would pass right by and not recognize them. Imagine if every piece had remembered that all its strange edges and colors were not always meant to make sense at first but that they carried within them a key to the cosmic puzzle.

It Was Real

It was real, you and I
I can tell by the way my heart aches
Even after all this time
When I hear your name
It is a wave crashing into me
I wonder if you feel the same
But I've learned to let you be
I was a temporary relief
From the pain trapped beneath your skin
Oh, what a lesson to have learned
The cost of being someone's medicine

Alone

To be alone is vastly different than to be lonely. Alone is a unique intimacy with all of life that can only be felt when the noise we normally cover silence with vanishes. To be alone is to let go of all those things you thought made up who you were, so that who you truly are finally has space to emerge. Alone is peaceful, empowering in fact. We can finally hear the voice of our own inner being and make choices from a place that is more authentic to the soul. Alone relies on no one and no thing for fulfillment, because something far deeper can be felt—the underlying current of life that connects us all.

The Mind's Garden

Rip out the weeds that
Were planted in your mind
When it was unaware
You decide what blooms inside of you,
And the sweetest rose must be cared for each day
(Your mind has been thirsty for your love)

Nostalgia for the Now

I feel a nostalgia for the present
Knowing I will never exist
Within the same moment
I am trying to learn all my lessons
Before this chapter of life
Comes to a closing
Everything I do not learn
Circles back wearing a different face
On my path, I seek to create new turns
The cost of this leaning into
The unknown's embrace

The Wolves

We all have two wolves inside of us
A wolf of the night and a wolf made from light
They tell me to be careful which one I feed
But if I am to feel at home within my skin
Am I not to love the duality within?
By understanding my dark wolf
I can understand yours
Instead of turning away in judgment
I recognize we're akin at our core
Allow your wolves to remain untamed
Like the river of life that runs in your veins

Love Will Never Ask You to Be Small

I squeezed into the small, dark places in you
Attempting to shine a light in your heart's cave
It was easier to try and heal your wounds
Than look at all the ways in which I had betrayed myself
I knew better than to be your medicine
To play the healer and the mother
We both failed at being each other's remedy
Shrinking is never the answer

Her

Have you ever wondered what lies beneath her smile?
Those eyes that strip you bare with a stare that runs you
wild. She has an inner mystery that cannot be touched.
Though many have tried to possess her, she is a rose that
cannot be plucked. She yearns for joy as the desert might
yearn for the rain. Yet she knows that to feel pleasure she
must learn not to run from her pain. It is far easier to find
a connection anchored on the surface, but she'll demand
you dive deep until you're living in your purpose. Do not
fear drowning when there is an entire ocean to explore.
You'll have to brave the dark waters, but I promise you'll
discover a life that is so much more.

For the Empaths

It's a gift, you know, to feel so deeply. To be sensitive is a unique superpower. Life may affect you in ways you may not have chosen for yourself. To see people as they are instead of the mirage presented . . . it's rare. And the world needs more rarities. So be someone who truly cares and makes time to listen. The sooner you stop wishing you were different, the sooner you can hone the special set of gifts only you have. Like a treasure hunt, we seek the gems inside ourselves to give them back to the world. And that only happens by coming to know yourself. By melting the armor we were taught to wear so young, and learning the strength it takes to be soft. Only then can we feel a piece of ourselves in every person. There is a balancing art in respecting where everyone is on their path while being patient with where we stand on our own.

The Desert Rose

Tell a woman she is beautiful
And she will forget it a moment later
Like a desert flower drowning in too much water
Whisper to her of her creativity, intelligence, and strength
And she will bloom under the hot sun
She will become a rare oasis
Breathing life into all who encounter her
The honeybee that kisses her mouth
Will carry her gift of love and pollinate the rest
   of the desert
Until it ripples out in a never-ending cycle
Next time, compliment something beyond her
   transient beauty
She bloomed in a harsh environment
So that you could live

Grief

Grief will come and steal your breath
It will have its way with you
Until you feel there's nothing left
I promise grief will one day leave
But not until the pain brings you to your knees

The Fingerprints You Left on My Heart

"Do you miss him?"
"Yes," she replied
You could see their memories
Flood across her eyes
True connections never end
Through time and distance
Her heart will mend
But a part of him
Will always exist within her

Open Your Eyes

That mind of yours that tells you to hide those wings
Because crawling would be safer
Quiet that voice for a moment
Let go of your grip on who you think you're supposed to be
If you borrowed my eyes you would weep at the sight
    of yourself
How much will it take before you remove that blindfold you
    were taught to wear and see even a fraction of what
    I see?

After

I once feared losing you and becoming lost in you
Though that is what happens when your heart is outside
    your chest
I went over it in my mind
How she repeated the same words you had once told me
Except this time I saw through your smoke screen
I loved you without asking for it in return
I forgave you without an apology for the bridge you burned
But this time you did not break my heart
You broke my trust
And that is something far more difficult to earn
Man is afraid of his own reflection
So he travels from woman to woman
Terrified of exploring the depths of a connection
When love is the greatest experience of being human

Love Is Not

If you want to alter the direction of your path for someone, it's not love. If you want to change your values for someone, it's not love. If you want to put your dreams on hold, compromise who you are, or swallow your truth for someone, it's not love. It's an unhealed part of you recognizing an unhealed part in them. Ironically, it is often the most passionate connection because of the intense familiarity. You have to see it for what it is. They're a lesson, not a soul mate. They aren't meant to fill the tears inside of you. They're meant to further rip those tears open so you give them an honest look and finally repair what was once broken. That way, when true love does come, you will truly love from wholeness. Your ability to heal will deepen your ability to love so that you do not reduce the other into being your medicine, distraction, or possession. Do not remold who you are. Remember: Love never demands you change. It only ever demands you become honest and whole.

A Smile Beneath the Surface

Growing up, my mother had a smile that never touched
   her eyes
And I prayed one day she would know true joy inside
When asked how she was, she would slip on the mask of
   radiance and say, "I'm fine."
She learned from generations of women taught to suppress
   the truth and hide
You see, my mother married her best friend
A man who would have sleepwalked through life with her
   until the very end
But she knew their love was no longer a home, it was a trap
Filled with the space of everything they avoided looking at
One day she remembered she is the creator of her life
And when she completely started over, I never
   questioned why
She curled up on the couch with a new man
And her smile reached her eyes as they lay there hand
   in hand
Death is so long when you look at our life span
She taught me to feel infinite within my finite life
And treat it as an adventure that is bold, joyous, and grand

Are You Nice or Kind?

There is a difference between being nice and being kind.
Nice can be dishonest. It can be a "yes" when we really
mean "no." Nice can be the perfect bandage for our true
feelings. Nice is normal—comfortable, in fact. It doesn't
shake up our beliefs or awaken deeper layers of knowing.
Nice floats along from place to place, denying the freedom
that comes with choice. Kindness is different. Kindness
takes strength. It takes honesty. Kindness will never ask
you to sacrifice your integrity; it will hold you to it. When
there has been wrongdoing, Nice will say, "It's fine!" with
a big smile and hollow eyes. Kindness will say, "This isn't
okay, and there needs to be a change, but I hold you with
compassion and understanding." Kindness knows the power
in honesty and how enabling people strips us of that
empowerment. Nice is taught, but kindness? Kindness is
who we innately are at our core.

The Sun in Your Chest

When your mind pulls you into the darkness of doubt,
I hope you ignite the unlit wick of your heart. After all
that life has thrown your way—the loss, the failure, the
heartbreak—have you allowed the wildfire buried in your
chest to be reduced to a candle flame? I often marvel at
how so much life can be contained by your delicate skin.
I hope when you reflect you see that not a single drop of
time has been wasted in any breath you have taken. Many
of our hearts have become unlit wicks, but for those who
remember the entire sun is within them, you'll feel the joy
in every word that spills from their lips. They treat the earth
as a drum beneath their dancing feet. They never grip
tightly to any outcome, knowing life always brings them
what they need.

Patterns Passed Down

I walked a mile in my ancestors' shoes
And felt all my mother and her mother had been through
Generations of women to be seen and not heard
Our inherited beliefs told us to hustle for our worth
Many lives had to be lived for me to be born
Their experiences are encapsulated in my cells
As I become aware of my past trauma, I repair what has
    been torn
These patterns end with me so my future daughter
Does not have the same story to retell

To the Weird Ones

And if numb is the new normal, then let me be the weird one. Let me be so moved that the simple sight of dawn breaks the silence of my soul in celebration. Let me become a blank canvas for life to paint on, for I am no longer interested in drawing perfect lines to live trapped within. Let me be forever changed by the stories that tumble from your trembling lips. Let me walk down the streets feeling naked from the inside out because I am no longer covering up who I am. Let me feel all of it. The raw and chaotic richness of life because normal would forever steal the light that dances in my eyes.

Masks

Last night I felt a heaviness in my chest
As the weight of our memories pressed upon my body
I asked Gravity to go bother someone else,
And she said, "If it is levity that you seek,
Unmask your sadness
And you will find anger
Unmask your anger
And you will find pain
Unmask your pain
And you will find joy."
I asked her if it was truly so simple, and she said,
"The problem is that most people forget they are wearing
    a mask to begin with."

Make Peace with Your Pieces

One day, she realized she could not outrun her shadow
She brought it in front of her where she could see it
"Why are you so dark?" she asked
Her shadow replied,
"Darkness is the truth you avoid, and
It yearns for the light."
Though it was painful to stand
In front of a silhouette of her unhealed pieces
She realized it was merely a part of her
That she had not made peace with
As she held herself in the love of her own arms
Her shadow became a part of her, like
The dusk of the setting sun melting into the night sky

Where Do You Wander?

If I asked you to tell me of heartbreak, your mind would probably wander to a past lover. But the truth is we break our own hearts long before we place them in the shaking hands of another. If I asked you to tell me of grief, you would think of the ones you have lost. The way the pain brings you to your knees, and there are no five stages for that depth of loss. If I asked you to tell me of worth, you may think only of its absence. Caught between feeling too much and not enough, waiting to become free from the story you're trapped in. If I asked you to tell me of beauty, you would most likely think of a person or place. But I have fallen in love with the sound of your laugh and the raw look of vulnerability I sometimes glimpse on your face.

Untamed

Feelings are like horses
It is best to allow them to run themselves wild
Instead of trying to tame their power
There will come a time when we all must choose
Between expressing ourselves
And suppressing ourselves

Let Go

Sometimes you don't realize
What you are holding on to
Until you let it go

You Are Strong

You are strong enough to forgive where others will
    simply resent
You are strong enough to set boundaries where others
    will be walked on
You are strong enough to be compassionate when others
    will simply judge
You are strong enough to embrace who you are where
    others will cover it up
You are strong enough to be soft where others will let life
    harden them
You are strong enough to love
You are strong
You are strong
You are strong

Wild Woman

What is the power of a wild woman?
Is it in the curve of her hips,
Or the knowing smile on her lips?
Is it in the strength of her thighs,
Or the sparkle in her eyes?
Is it in the history her back wears,
Or her untamed hair?
Is it in her sensitivity,
Or the way her unpredictable emotions
Teach us to speak the language of creativity?
Is it in how deep her love runs,
Or the way she and the moon's cycles are one?
Every month she experiences death
Shedding all the shadow her body has kept
The power of a wild woman
Runs through the woman
Who remembers her worth
Who recognizes her body as a portal
Through which life makes birth
A wild woman does not spend her sacred energy
Apologizing for who she is
But instead reminds other women
Of their own wild nature
Through taking care of herself

She knows she can genuinely give
She does not soften her voice
Or suppress what is truly her heart's choice
The more I come to know the wild woman
The less I can explain her through words
So perhaps if you close your eyes
And withdraw from the world outside
Her guidance will be heard

Home

Your mind is the house you live in
But most people do not see it this way
And so they chase the things they think they need to have
Not realizing what you have can be lost in a moment
But what you are can never be taken
And so I ask you: Is your mind a palace or a prison?
Do not fear the house of cards you built crumbling
Once that pretty ceiling is gone
You will be able to drink in the stars in the quiet of the night
And finally hear the silent invitation of your heart as she
    whispers softly,
"Come dance with me."

Ouroboros

Have you ever seen a snake
Rush her shedding process?
She moves through each phase
With fluidity and grace
Though the death of
Her old skin can be ugly
This too she knows to embrace

Digital Disconnection

How strange it is to live in a world so rich in distraction
and yet poor in meaningful interaction. The double tap on
your screen will never replace the warmth that comes from
feeling the double beat of your heart. I suppose we are
living in a time that values being admired over being loved.
Yet finding fulfillment in this way is on par with catching
mist—you may feel something for a brief moment, but in
the end you'll always be thirsting for more.

The Lion Inside

There is a lion inside of you
And she wants to be free
I have seen glimpses of her wildness
When you forget to pull her leash
I have acted as prey
Trying to tempt her to be released
But you have muzzled her roar
Barely giving her enough air to breathe
Why do we fear the lion inside us being untamed?
When she holds the courageous power
We need to break free and change
I have no interest in living
A half-life where my lion is trapped
She intuitively guides me in
Following my soul's map
Her roar is far louder than
The whispers of my fear
I beg you to release your lion
And claim the love that has always been here!

Kindness

Do not mistake my kindness for weakness
As one might mistake the gentle elephant for being tamed
A heart that stays open even when it hurts
Is the heart willing to make the hard choice
Because it knows it is the right choice

Alive

I have no interest in being a creature of habit. But if I am to be habitual, then let my routine be one of seeking all that forces me to stretch. Let me seek what makes my blood race until I feel lightning strike my chest as this thundering heartbeat reminds me what the word "alive" really means. Underneath every fear is simply fear itself. And if death is to greet us all at one time or another, then I will return to the ground with a smile on my face in hopes that the grass that grows from my bones may become the floor that someone else dances on.

Ebb and Flow

If woman is the moon
And man is the sea
No wonder he avoids her love
Her energy is like a magnet
That creates chaos within his tides
Until the order of his waves
No longer make sense
Oh, but we forget happiness
Was never meant to be organized

He Was a Lesson Dressed as Love

Allow him to become a memory
He was a part of you that needed to be felt
But your paths are now on different trajectories
To hold on would be to wear the mask of your old self
Smile at his memory, then let it go
Allow space for new love to grow
One day you may circle back around
And laugh at the days when you both wondered
When you would feel found
You are love hiding from yourself
And you looked for it in him
So of course it fell apart!
Didn't anyone tell you love is found within?

Betrayal

Sometimes a lesson may wear the face of betrayal
And you may ask yourself, "How could this have happened
    to me?"
Remember they betrayed themselves long before they
    betrayed you
Do not wield their mistake like a sharpened blade
Cutting them as they have cut you
This will not mend your wounds
They feel more pain inside
Than you could ever inflict
Find the love to let them go
For that is the same love
That will set you free

Fly

We do not choose who we fall in love with
But if they are not ready to meet you on the edge
Let them go and do not try to fix their broken wings
They must fall in love with their own beating heart
Before they can finally fly with you
And I promise one day
You will meet someone who leaps without question

Social Masks

There was once a fish who wandered the desert for miles
It tried so very hard to keep up with the camels
Each day it pressed on through an ocean of dry sand
Wondering why everything felt so wrong
Until they reached the desert's edge
And in front of them stretched the sea
The fish dove beneath the water
Breathing for the first time
Feeling it was finally home

Your World Is Your Perception of the World

Remember something, my love,
This reality is a brilliant trick of the senses
Do not take yourself so seriously
All our atoms dance to their own song
Do not waste your one precious life
Trying to follow someone else's tune
Can you hear it?
Can you hear your unique song?

All Truths Exist Within a Paradox

My heart chases nothing for it knows that it is everything
My mind chases everything for it fears that it is nothing
My soul knows that everything comes from nothing

Lens of Two

I laugh at myself for looking
At my world through a lens of two
For believing the story that I was finally worthy of love
Because I was with you

This Too Is Happening for You

Sometimes you must let go of your pieces
For things to come back together
Trust, my love, what was is not for you
And what will be is always better
If you are brave enough to follow the voice
That is guiding you to your heart's treasure
You'll make every decision a mindful choice
That will lead you to a love greater than you can measure

The Free Spirit

It is beautiful to be free-spirited, but do not make the mistake of becoming attached to being nonattached. Freedom is not found in floating from person to person, in being an enigma incapable of being tied down. Let's not romanticize it. That is avoidance. A fear that, when exploring the depths of a connection with the same people, we will have to face our own reflection. And we will, but that is where true freedom exists. Create meaningful connections with people who see you for the parts you love about yourself and the parts you are terrified of revealing. A truly free spirit is aware of their own shadow and willing to face it. They understand love takes time. That unshakeable trust is earned in everyday moments. Be brave enough to sink a little deeper with the people in your life. I promise you, they are the greatest treasures you will ever come across. They create the opportunity to understand and be understood.

Expectations

"Why do relationships fall apart?" he asked.
"Expectations," she replied.

The Questions

I have known those who say they have the answers
But I prefer to surround myself with those who live
   the questions
I have known those who are the picture of success
Prisoners to their own perfection
Instead of learning to love their mess
I have known those who are afraid to commit their hearts
The luxury of so many choices
Paralyzes them from even knowing where to start
I have known those who embody great joy
They do not run from sorrow
And there is no part of themselves they wish to destroy
I have known those who understand their life to be
   an adventure
A brief opportunity to experience Earth
They understand true love lies in surrender

Once Upon a Time

Once upon a time
A woman slipped into a world of dreams
Where all she had to do was what society told her
But in her heart she knew life was not as it seemed
So she refused to allow the world to mold her
They told her to wait for a prince to help her awaken
But she was no sleeping beauty
And would never allow her strength to be taken

Mirror, Mirror, on the Wall

Mirror, mirror, on the wall,
One day I will learn to stand proud and tall,
I will see my curves as poetry wrapped in skin
The first thing I notice will be the wild soul within
Mirror, mirror, on the wall,
Why did I ever try and change myself at all?
The standard of beauty I try to meet
Is a waste of energy when my value runs more than
    skin-deep
Mirror, mirror, on the wall,
I will learn self-love even if I stumble and fall
From the time of my daughter's birth
I promise you this
I will make sure that she never forgets her worth

I Would Have Loved You

I would have loved you,
In another life, when the time was right
I would have loved you,
Under the cover of the night, when you let down all
    your walls
I would have loved you,
But in order to love, you have to let yourself fall
I would have loved you,
For it would be the sweetest of connections
But now, my love, I do not seek comfort
I seek an awakening reflection
I would have loved you,
But you chose to love me when I was ready to leave you
I would have loved you,
But now it is time for me to go
I will always love you,
And because of this, I release you, so we both can
    finally grow

Nothing Is Worth Closing Your Heart Over

There is a fear that keeps me alive
And a fear that keeps me from living
Like a rose that blooms in the night
Out of darkness can come the most beautiful beginnings
The gates of my rib cage are open
Enter my heart anytime
My walls of protection are broken
Through vulnerability I stand in the light
Many tell me to put a lock on my gate
To protect my body's greatest treasure
And it is true, love can hurt
But I will never close off to pain
For this is life's greatest pleasure

Show Me Honesty

Show me an honest anger over a dishonest peace. Show me a person honestly accountable for their mistakes over a dishonest perfection. Show me the person who doesn't claim to have the answers. Show me the person who, instead of saying, "This is the path," says, "Go inside and discover where your path leads you." Show me the person who is not afraid to do the ugly cry instead of wear a smile on their face that doesn't reach their eyes. Honest self-love doesn't look like a bubble bath or chocolate cake. Honest self-love is when the most human part of us that we feel guilty or ashamed of gets triggered, and we can look ourselves square in the eyes without judgment because our love is not conditional. We can be brave enough to become aware of our own bullshit, so that we can grow into more accepting and loving human beings. I have a lot to learn in this life. If I know something, it is that none of us escapes being human. But an honest human is capable of an honest love.

You're Worth It

you're worth it, I tell you
you're worth walking that path you are so uncertain of
the path toward what you love and fear most
walk it trembling if you must
but keep placing one foot in front of the other
you're worth it, I tell you
you're worth healing
not because you need to be fixed
but so that you can know what it is
to feel free inside once the weight of your pain is gone
you're worth it, I tell you
you're worth the kind of love
that forces you to be courageous in your own life
the kind of love that is relentless in its demand
for your most honest and wonderfully weird self
you're worth it, I tell you
you're worth following that beating compass in your chest
as it guides you on that path with your name on it
you are the knight on the horse and the hero in the cape
    you've been waiting for

Part 2: Dawn

A Tale of Two Lovers

When I woke up from my dream
My feet were bruised
From wandering the galaxy
I danced on Saturn's rings
And swam in the depths
Of Neptune's ocean
More stars swirled around me
Than I had ever seen
I lay down within
A bed of constellations
And observed this strange, blue planet
I turned to the Sun, who smiled at me
"What is this place?" I asked him
The Sun replied, "It is called Earth. My love breathes life
    into her."
Confused, I said, "But you're so very far away."
The Sun sighed, "We must allow the things we love
    absolute freedom."

Love's Rhythm

That instrument you call a heart
Have you played it lately?
Have you created music
For your loved ones to dance to?
Or is your instrument a little out of tune
Gathering dust?
I know how your starving heart gets
When you live in a world without music

Contradictions

Be a walking contradiction. Be strong and soft. Be silly and sincere. Be deep and lighthearted. Be beautiful and intelligent. Be confident and humble. Be content climbing a mountain and enjoying the sweetness of doing nothing. The world may try and classify you as one thing because that is far easier to understand than a person who has a little bit of everything in them. And you may feel misunderstood for a while, but just remember your people can only find you if you're brave enough to be yourself. There are parts of you that you have yet to discover. There is greater love that you have yet to find. There are experiences that are far beyond your imagination. And it's all waiting for you. Life is waiting for you. Set aside your expectations and go explore it.

Disconnection

When did cell reception
Replace human connection?
When did "likes" start validating
Our worth on the planet
Notifications numbing us with dopamine
Until our problems seemingly vanish?
It all comes back to what we seek lying within
Not a number in our bank account
Or the feeling of a lover against our skin
I'll tell you a secret: you'll never feel you have arrived
So fall in love with the process
And learn from life's every surprise
It's not about how many goals we hit
But the growth that comes from showing up for
    each moment
And embracing life for what it is
The moments I remember most are
Free of social masks and games
When I feel home within vulnerability
And remember underneath our identities we're the same
Though it appears much easier to protect ourselves
    through isolation
I promise you this:
True love will never be matched by instant gratification

Before the One

When you think you have found the one
And it feels close to love
But not quite right
Let them go
That is the one before the one

What Are You Influencing?

Imagine our people as one whole body
I am the heart and you are the lungs
Your mother the strong spine
The man on the street the legs that carry us
Each person playing an essential role
But what if I said I was only going to look out for myself?
Look what happens with a love like that
The rest of the organs fail from a heart that forgot
The effect every beat has on the rest of us

Fall in Love with the Process

I admire the soft and the subtle. The ones who care far too much and feel far too deeply. You see, I have fallen in love with your imperfections. When you let go of that tight grip on who you think you should be and fully embrace all that you're becoming. In some form or another, we're all a little lost inside, because the future is an unanswerable question. Don't rush your blooming—the process of growth is what makes life so mysteriously enticing. Remember all that it has taken for you to arrive in this moment. The lives that came before you. The experiences that you have been through. The inherited wisdom that whispers softly to you when you stop covering up the silence. Can't you see that those quirks you've been hiding are what make you so wonderfully unique?

The Nature of Love

Love is never based in fear
It does not try to control
Love accepts you as you are right here
And reflects how you're already whole
Sometimes we are drawn to another
From a matching wound
Looking to externally heal our past
But love will never consume
Infatuation and passion are not strong enough to last
Though love can remove any barrier
It asks that we first take off our masks
Love holds your heart in gentle hands
It will never hold it captive
You must leave if it begins to make demands
Before your soft heart hardens from the pain impacted

Begin Again

Little by little, you will begin to understand a fresh start is not marked by a day but rather belongs to you at any and all moments. Little by little, you will discover that there is a whole world inside of you, and we'll laugh together at how you once believed in that lie called limitation. Little by little, you will fall deeply in love with life until a sparkle of passion is permanently painted in your eyes. Little by little, you will feel the magic that exists in you. Little by little, you'll stop placing expectations on the blank pages ahead when you realize your story will be the most beautiful surprise for its every twist, turn, and triumph. This is your now. This is your year. This is your life.

Femme

There's something about the way her spirit seems to escape her body in all her wildness. As though there is far too much life in her to ever be contained to mere flesh. Even now as I try to piece together the words to describe her, I'll never be able to weave together a sentence that matches the feelings she sparks. It is something like looking a jaguar square in the eyes—beautiful to admire from a distance, but up close your very nerves are on fire with the uncertainty of what she will do next. I don't know that she could ever belong to anyone, except perhaps Mother Nature herself.

What I Know Is That I Do Not Know

Who you are
Is what you understand
And what you understand
Is in your understanding
Of how much you do not understand
Do you understand?

Freedom to Fail

I would rather fail doing what I love
Than hide behind the success of what feels safe
Trying to avoid judgment and failure
Is akin to shackling your wings
This life is not very long, you see
It may feel like a great risk to put your heart in the ring
With your dreams so vulnerably exposed on the line
The greatest risk of all would be to never even try
Don't you see?
If you fail doing what you love,
It is not failure at all

Death Creates Life

When Death comes for me,
I will greet him with a smile
I hope he finds me dancing with laughter
Because each moment I lived was worthwhile
When Death comes for me,
I will greet him as a friend
Without him I would not have lived so wildly
You only see your journey as precious if there is an end
When Death comes for me,
I'll keep my memories close to my heart
Knowing I was brave to feel so deeply
Creating a life that is a work of art
When Death comes for me,
I'll laugh at all my worries
My time on this spinning blue ball was a wink of eternity,
And none of my fears were ever truly worthy
When Death comes for me,
I'll think of everyone I have ever loved,
Knowing all else in life is a bonus
But connection is what matters when push comes to shove

The Bookend of Breath

Between your first and last breath
Is the story that you create
Think of the biggest twists and turns
That have led you to your current state
When we learn from our past
We become free from the unconscious acts we play
Pay close attention to the eternal now
Trust your heart will never lead you astray

Maybe She's More Than Enough

Maybe her dress is a little wrinkled and her hair always out of place. Maybe she doesn't need to seek perfection to live her life with grace. Maybe some days it seems she has swallowed the sun with her smile. Maybe other days she allows herself to fall apart for a while. Maybe some moments she enjoys the sweetness of doing nothing. Maybe other moments she races toward her dreams until she can touch them. Maybe she understands the never-ending lesson of being human. Maybe she understands a seed is planted in darkness before it begins blooming. Maybe she knows all of the love life can give. Maybe she knows that a life without love is not one that has been lived.

The Right Person at the Wrong Time

I asked what you were thinking
You smiled and looked at the rain
The right person at the wrong time
Will cause a lot of pain
The man he would one day be
Was the man I was looking for
But I had already learned that lesson
So to that moment I closed the door
Loving someone for their potential
Only hurts their growth and yours
Keep blooming and trust your process
There is a love that is so much more

Love Without Reason

Love without reason. Love because it took at least 13 billion years for you to even come into existence. Love so that we stop raising broken people who spread the pain they feel on the world. Love because that is your nature, and your heart doesn't need to feel the gravity that comes with holding on to things. You may have been wounded in the past, but do you need to wear the story of those wounds? Love so that you can let go. Love so that you can truly live.

Trust Your Pace

My soul was made of the wind
I never know where she will guide me
Sometimes she is barely a soft breeze
Others she swirls in a new direction
So fast my mind spins in confusion
Though I think this is her point
To give my heart a running head start

What Is Meant for You Cannot Miss You

To love someone who is not ready for you
Is to drag a man who does not know how to swim
Into the deepest part of the ocean
(Do not drown another out of loneliness)

Is Your Love for Yourself Conditional?

I never needed you to be perfect. I needed you to be
yourself. To not bury the broken bits of you beneath
a smile, or look for the glue to your pieces in the heart
of another. It's a terrible thing, really, to love yourself
conditionally. To only allow the feeling of joy in when you
have met your own standards. Here's the unfiltered truth:
you're never going to be perfect, nor will you find a person
who is perfect. Perfect is an idea we tell ourselves that
exists in the future. You can always become stronger,
smarter, richer, more successful, more beautiful. So when
does it end? When do you decide you're worthy of your
own unconditional love? No one is ever ready for anything,
but if you are to truly experience the world within your
one precious life, you'd better decide to open your heart
and let each moment take your breath away. You can
get to anywhere you want to be from where you're
standing, but can't you see that where you're standing
is already beautiful?

Holding Space

The hard shell of every person can be cracked open
Through a gentle ear
I have found listening to be
The most potent form of medicine

Codependency

He left breadcrumbs that my starving heart
Pretended were an exquisite entrée
He knew if he left a little at a time
I would stay from fear of having nothing at all
Only when I began to nourish myself
Would I no longer accept his scraps

Hollow Nectar

Honey may drip from his lips when he speaks
Drawing you in with the promise of nectar so sweet
My queen, have you forgotten that
You are the flower that creates the life he seeks?
Do not settle for beautifully woven words
That mask the hollowness underneath
There are others who will value the love that you give
And know how to pollinate a flower
Whose value extends beyond fleeting moments of bliss

One

When people ask me where I am from
I always reply, "Earth"
I do not separate myself
Based on invisible lines drawn in dirt
I celebrate diversity
But do not let it divide
We're all students in life's university
And bleed the same color inside

Stillness

I'm always looking for quiet places where the chaotic dance
of the world halts and in stillness I hear nothing but the
sound of my own breath. I feel the muddy earth beneath
my feet and the soft drum of a heart so alive beating in
my chest. Time stretches as I become comfortable with
space. That's the key—not to fill yourself with what is not
meant for you out of a fear of emptiness. I wonder how we
keep that silence within, or if we're meant to let go and join
the chaotic dance.

It Was Always Within You

You already contain all that you seek
The only thing holding you captive is your beliefs
Allow love's fire to burn away what is no longer true
Until all that is left is the rawest version of you

When I Have a Daughter

When I have a daughter,
I will make sure she knows
That she is a miraculous portal life can come through
I will make sure she knows
That her body is to be loved and cherished
I will make sure she knows
That her intuition is to be trusted and followed
I will make sure she knows
That she is never to tame her wild
I will make sure she knows
That her brilliance and her beauty are one and the same
I will make sure she knows
Never to apologize for who she is if she lives with love
    and integrity
I will make sure she knows
A strong "no" before an uncertain "yes"
I will make sure she knows
That the love within herself is stronger than any prince

Honest Moments

Keep the honest moments close to your heart. The ones that are the most human. When you laugh until your ribs ache with your friends, when you feel stars exploding inside of you from falling in love, when life breaks you open and those tears of transformation pour like a river from your soul. Life is really quite simple. We get to experience this planet for a brief while. We get to learn how to love ourselves and one another for the strange, messy, and magical creatures we are. What a gift it is to have a human life. If you look a little closer, there is always something to be grateful for. True gratitude does not mean ignoring the darkness. True gratitude means participating with your whole heart in whatever moment life brings. It means leaning into the unfolding process, and having the courage to not need all of the answers.

How Will You Respond?

This world is a lot to swallow
But the one thing it cannot take from you
Is how you respond to every situation
And if I know one thing, it's this:
It takes far more strength to respond with love

Brave

There was once a boy who could not speak his truth
He buried how he felt so that his love never knew
He did not realize that she loved him too
And they went their whole lives
Never having a clue

Allie Michelle

My Heart Holds the Reins

Someone can know better and still not do better
I felt our relationship expire
I knew holding on meant holding both of us back
We fall in love with who we need to learn from
The one who will challenge and change us
My mind knew from the start we wouldn't last
But my heart has always held the reins in this body of mine
So I let her run me wild with the experience of loving you

The Chase

You are chasing a life that is not meant for you, my love
That is why you are in so much pain
When you stop running so fast
Your purpose will finally have time to catch up with you

For the One Who Gave It All

There are going to be times when your path isn't clear.
There are going to be times when it feels as though the pain
may never end. There are going to be times when nothing
makes sense. There are going to be times when your life
is upside down and you wonder if you'll ever be able to find
the ground again. Keep breathing. Keep going. Keep
walking the path. Keep taking a step each day toward your
healing. I promise you will one day live your way into feeling
whole again, and when you look back you'll see why
everything happened the way that it did. You'll see how
every moment led to this one. There is nothing life sends
your way that you cannot breathe through. Your heart may
be shattered, but do not close it, sweet soul. It is far too
precious to wilt under someone who was never capable of
watering it in the first place. Confront all that is haunted
within you and let the pain in so that you can let the pain
out. One day those ghosts will be nothing but a story you
tell as you sit, surrounded by those who love you, with a
smile on your face. One day, when you see someone else
with this kind of heaviness in their chest, you will be able
to speak straight to their strength and remind them that
there is nothing that is broken that cannot be rebuilt.

Social Media

I scroll through my feed and wish I had my life
I watch as people lose their worth comparing followers
    and likes
They tell you that you will be successful
If you become more like them
But your power comes from the unique ways that you're you
I have never done well at fitting into a square box
I compare my squares to theirs
And all of a sudden I feel lost
Then there is the pressure to constantly produce perfect art
It is forgotten instantly and then you're right back at
    the start
How can I be original in a space with so much noise?
I suppose all I really have is my own authentic voice
It is a dangerous game that we're all playing
Chasing money, chasing fame
And finding our true selves
But if a flower worried about instant gratification
She would never have time to bloom
So turn off your phone
Put your hands on your heart
And give yourself some room
I promise that is more real than the content you consume

Become the Love You Wish You Had Found

Become the love you wish you had found in him
Why do you look for love
In the one person who cannot give it to you?
Emotional unavailability is not something to be drawn to
You have not gone through
The pain and pressure of becoming a diamond
Only to accept someone
Who believes themselves to still be coal

Seek to Love Before You Seek to Understand

Seek to love people before you seek to understand them.
Everyone is on their own private journey with an entire
world inside of them that we will never fully come to know.
We can go through the same experience together, but
that moment will mean something entirely different to
each of us. As we weave in and out of each other's paths,
people will surprise us in a million ways. Some ways will hurt
us and some ways will heal us. Some ways will challenge
us and some ways will change us. What if each person is
just a teacher, a looking glass that mirrors to us the two
wolves within? Without tension there would never be
any growth. Conflict in nature is what creates islands,
canyons, and supernovas that birth new worlds. So
remember that when your heart cracks in your chest, it is
not broken. It is letting the light in.

Between Two Worlds

We are the bridge
Between eternity and the world of time
Presence is a brief glimpse above the clouds
Where we can feel the warmth
Of the golden sun on our skin
Before returning into the fog of the mind
We walk between two worlds
Balancing the magic and the mundane

The Beginning

And so one day it happened like this. I was floating amongst an ocean of stars in timeless space. All it took was one look from Earth and she cast her line, hooking me into her orbit. Never had I seen such unparalleled beauty than in the life that dwelled within her gravitational currents. I asked if I could experience a human life. To know the feeling of a mortal heart that feels immortal in love, or the peace that washes over from being submerged in the salty sea, or the enveloping scent of a bonfire from camping beneath pine trees. I wanted to physically experience the chaotic dance of emotions that makes a human life so rich. Earth granted me my wish and asked which character I would like to play when I came in. I made up a name and many other ingredients that would create my story so that I could grow along the way. She said the price of admission was that I would experience amnesia. I would forget that I came from infinity, and instead identify with the role I play, thinking that it was me. Part of the game was participating in the mystery. A treasure hunt of following the breadcrumbs, and soft whispers of inspiration that reminded me of the endless possibilities contained within one human life.

Why Bother Creating?

Life does not make art possible
Art makes life possible
The artist and the alchemist are the same
They are masters who use every experience
As an opportunity to create change
They make art that captures the feelings
We cannot put into words
Art that is made honestly
Allows a misunderstood heart to feel heard

Soul Mates

There are some people you meet,
And you sense your atoms have danced together before
They will feel like home and a grand adventure all at once
With eyes that see far too deeply,
They understand the language of your heart
That you thought only you spoke
Between our first inhale and our last exhale
The depth of the story in between
Is marked by the depth of the connections we have
Becoming whole may be lonely at first
But when you embrace who you truly are,
You'll find people who accept the honest you. The messy
   you. The strong you.
As you're embraced with more love than you've ever felt
You'll look into their eyes and see reflected back your
   true self

Humble

Coming home to myself is like walking
A thin tightrope over the Grand Canyon
Gratification sways me one way
Failure sways me another
I used to crave the first
But either way in which I'm swayed
Leads me to an empty abyss
I have fallen and pulled myself up
Too many times to want anything but inner stillness

Accountability

Karma whispered softly in my ear and said, "Every story you tell yourself about another person is a trick of perspective. We all have our ways of chasing love and happiness. Dehumanizing another does not more deeply humanize you. So treat people better than you have been treated. We fall in love with those who carry lessons for us. An open heart will always feel deeply to the core. Let love's crackling embers burn away all that is built up inside, until there is a peaceful emptiness within. Like a hollow instrument, each moment will be music that is played through you."

The Man Who Caged His Creativity

There is a man who lives in a congested, tired town where rent is expensive and success comes by the dollar. Each day he hustles for his worth in backdoor deals sealed by handshakes of paper-thin people dressed in white collars. Each night he comes home and lets his heart out of its cage, allowing it to fly. He paints, makes sculptures, and weaves stories together through the thread of his imagination. But then the first hints of the sun begin to appear in the starless sky, signaling tomorrow has arrived. So he quietly places his heart back in its cage and ties his tie around his neck, making sure it is nice and straight, leaving no traces of his wild nature as he goes to work.

When I Have a Son

When I have a son,
I will make sure he knows
That being a man does not mean being hard
I will make sure he knows
That a life lived with a closed heart is not a life lived at all
I will make sure he knows
That he must allow the full expression of his emotions in
    a healthy way
I will make sure he knows
That he does not need to hustle for his worth
I will make sure he knows
That a woman must be treated with the respect of a rose
    that blooms in the night
I will make sure he knows
Never to touch her soft petals without permission
I will make sure he knows
The strength it takes to be soft

The Only Words That Matter

My father called me his sunshine
He said my smile lit up every room
Then I grew up and into "real life"
Now I'm not sure what happened to the little girl he knew
He always wore a far-off look
As though he had one foot in another world
He was a quiet man
A quiet man who loved his daughters when all they wanted
    was to be let into that world
On Valentine's Day, that gentle heart that showed me the
    meaning of kindness
Slowed its beat until he was brought to his knees and could
    barely breathe
He crawled up three flights of stairs to the woman he had
    once called home for 33 years
So she could save the heart she broke
I still remember the sound of silence on the other end of
    the phone when I answered my mother's call
She choked on her words, and I stopped hearing after
    "heart attack"
Next was the sound of my beat-up tires screeching as I
    raced through traffic
Until I could place my hands in the ones that had carried
    me all my life

When he finally opened his eyes, all either of us could say
    was, "I love you"
And suddenly I realized this quiet man had always said the
    only words that mattered
I love you
I love you
I love you

The Answers Are in the Questions

Every day, she asked Life the same questions:
"What does this mean?"
"Why am I here?"
"Where am I going?"
"Will everything work out?"
Exasperated by her questions, Life came down and handed her a book. "This book has your entire future inside of it. Every twist and turn, love and loss, success and failure, down to the last detail until your death. Read it if you wish." Life walked away, leaving her with her future in the palm of her hands. She looked at the closed book for a while, feeling its weight. She could open it and know every little detail, down to when she would die. She realized that sometimes the answers exist within the questions themselves, and a world without mystery was a world without hope. She surrendered the book back into Life's hands, along with the worry that had consumed her mind.

The Danger of Doubt

Doubt is like a thief in the night who sneaks through the back door of your mind. He steals the dreams and ideas that dance across your imagination before you even dare bring them into reality. Doubt wears the mask of logic, telling you it has all been done before, so it is best not to allow your heart to be crushed under the weight of failure. You can write that book next year. You can make that movie or paint that painting when you have the money to buy back your time. Doubt has forgotten that creativity is not a career, it is nourishment that is essential to our being. When he sneaks into your mind, catch him in the act with your awareness before he reduces the magic to the mundane.

A False Promise in Your Eyes

You grabbed my chin
With your callused hands
And ran your thumb across my bottom lip
As you kissed me slowly,
I was amazed at how someone so strong
Could be so heartbreakingly gentle all at once
The look in your eyes held the promise
Of a thousand more moments like this
Sometimes I imagine a world
Where our love did not slip through your fingertips

Why Worry?

Worry is like trying to extinguish a fire with gasoline
It ignites the never-ending spiral of anxiety
Making a false promise that we can think our way out
    of the pain
When the future is a question that can never be answered
Instead of worrying, have you tried taking a deep breath,
    my love?

Speak Your Truth

I opened my mouth to cry
And the sound of a thousand silenced ancestors
Ripped through my vocal cords
(Your voice is a gift)

Conscious Love

You worshipped me with your tongue
And a thousand flowers bloomed between my legs
There is a world inside of me
You whispered softly in my ear
A promise of love
I heard the surrender in your tone
As you let go of the pressures of being a hard man
And simply melted into me like nectar
Give a woman your undivided presence
And watch her unfold

Love Simply to Love

Love simply to love. People may cause pain or act unconsciously at times, but that is coming from a wound that existed long before you crossed their path. Love simply to love. Everyone has their messy, human ways of being. Judging any of it is a waste of your one and only precious life, and trying to change people is about as useful as trying to contain the seven seas in a teacup. You'll drown in the attempt. So love simply to love. You deserve to feel free, and I mean truly free. Free of expectations, free of taking anything personally, free of worry, free of judgment. Love and freedom is your nature, and when you start to embody that, something amazing happens. The world will open its heart as you open yours. Colors will become brighter. Food will taste better. Everything will become a meaningful experience when you love simply to love.

Every Heart Simply Wishes to Be Heard

When every honest word
Is caught in your throat
It is the poet's job to become the voice for what you
    cannot say
Every heart simply wishes to be heard
As it dances like a drum 108,000 beats per day
We have 108,000 opportunities to listen
But perhaps the thought of feeling
Is too much

Revolving Door

My life is not a revolving door
You cannot expect to walk into a house that you once
   burned to ash
It took me a long time to rebuild upon what you broke
And this time I will not let you in so easily
My keys are to be earned

Are You in Love with Your Now?

It is bittersweet when you realize
You are living the memories
You will look back on and wish you could return to
My nostalgia for the present often haunts me
I know I will never live the same moment twice
And yet this is the price that comes with a human life
How priceless is it to live in a world where every moment
   is temporary?

This is the one and only time the sweet rose that is you
Will bloom in this way

The Danger of Victimization

We are all responsible for our beliefs
Yet we victimize ourselves for temporary relief
Not realizing the poison this spreads
Since we're all connected in an intricate web
I am accountable only to the edges of my skin
I cannot control what you learn and take in
I must live with my own energy anytime I judge
Letting go is much better than gripping onto a grudge
Our evolution is on its own clock
And only we can choose to open our locks

The Maze

Your path will be found as you walk blinded in the darkness,
stumbling until you learn to see through the eyes of your
heart. We are all lost in a maze called life, with pieces of
ourselves scattered throughout. As you walk your path,
you pick up those pieces of yourself along the way,
becoming whole with each lesson. And as we all know with
mazes, the path is never a straight line. No one can tell you
for certain what is the right way, and only you can take
a step on your journey. But remember, my love, life only
ever asks for one step at a time. You can take the long
way or you can learn your lessons with a hard shortcut.
Whichever route you take, you will learn and love until
you are whole within all your pieces again.

Just Love

And if you remember anything,
Let it be this:
Above all else, just love
It is the simple joys of living
That are the most fulfilling

One Year

It has been one year. One year since I first looked into your blue eyes that seemed to contain within them the entire sea. One year since I placed my heart in your shaking hands. It has been one year of growing and healing. One year of finding strength in my bones. One year of learning to become a force of nature. One year of understanding what self-love really means and how to never betray or abandon myself again. One year of discovering the power of a soft heart that could have so easily hardened. You became a memory, a part of the story I told. But when I saw you again, it was as though all the life that had happened in between dissolved. You were the same person I had always known. What surprised me was how different I felt. I did not expect to see my change reflected in your eyes.

Everyone Is the Teacher

Imagine if every soul you meet is one of your guides
Look deeper and you may recognize them
Beneath their human disguise
Every person is a reflection of your perspective
Mirroring how much you have grown
Through a web of synchronicity we are deeply connected
With each lesson learned we're bringing each other home
Pay close attention to the language of the heart
You'll hear its whisper in silence
If you're present enough, you'll experience life as a work
   of art
The return to love will shatter our confinements

Selective Memory

People love to the depths that they are able
Maybe their depth
Is your surface
It is far too easy to paint over the darkness of our memories
And selectively remember the beautiful parts of someone
If they are meant for you, they will be with you

Silence

We are always covering up silence
Wondering why we cannot hear the answers we seek
It is life's grand joke to have you search everywhere
    but here
Looking for love in different places and faces
When it has always existed in the moment
Close your eyes and listen

Seconds

Every second you spend being anyone but yourself
Is a second you deprive the world of your unique gifts

For Ida

My grandmother called me her little one
Though she looked at me as though I were anything
    but little
As though she saw the size of my heart mirrored her own
And the same river of strength ran in my blood
She taught me how to dine like a lady and play poker in the
    same day
She forced me to sit for Shabbat dinners
But then would sneak me ice cream instead of matzah
That was her, you see
Full of contradictions and the stubborn refusal
To let anyone tell her who she is
She was fiercely gentle
And had a sparkle of joy permanently painted on her eye
But beneath that sparkle there was worry
Never for herself, no
She was worried for her family
Always thinking of their happiness
As though she could be the sun, the water, and the fertilizer
    that made them bloom
If only she knew she did not have to be all things
Because the truth was her love was everything
I hope to find a fraction of her strength in myself

Don't You See?

Don't you see? This life is what you make it. Whether you go right or left, you're still on this human journey for a short while, floating in timeless space. And maybe you didn't choose where you came from or how it is you got here. But you're here. You made it. Never forget that, at any moment, you can decide to get up and walk away. You can explore a new place, learn a new skill, find a new love—it's all just an experience. The only tragic thing would be to find yourself sleepwalking through the miracle that is your life. If you chase what is not meant for you, that pain of "what if?" will always weigh heavily on your chest.

Passion

Follow what makes you lose track of time
When you do what you love
You will feel eternity stirring within you

Surprise

Believe me when I tell you
Nothing is ever as it seems
Life will surprise you in every possible way
And just when you think you know where you're going
You will find yourself tossed miles in another direction
Though it may all appear random
You will look back one day
And see how every experience was essential
In leading you to this one

Love Is a Reminder

People may surprise or hurt you
But never stop seeing the good in them
Those are not rose-colored lenses you wear
They are God's glasses
And She has lent them to you for this lifetime
So you can remind people of their true nature

Freedom

Do you feel free?
You can have absolutely everything
And feel like a prisoner within your own skin
Are you understanding now?
How your outer world is shaped by your inner world
What is the cost of that smile, my love?
Being the sun for everyone else means nothing
When you still feel pain inside
All the ways you judge yourself are starving your flames
    of oxygen
Face the darkness and let your light burn

Trust

My trust in you broke like shattered glass
A million pieces lost that once made something sacred
I looked into your eyes
As the pain of your betrayal flooded across them
And my anger melted away
How could I have expected someone so broken to be the
    glue to my pieces?

Select Your Thoughts

I left the door to my mind unlocked
Letting you walk into my home with mud all over your feet
And so now I scrub every corner of my mind
Until all thoughts of you are gone and I finally feel free

Love Is

If you asked me what love is
I would spend a lifetime trying to put it into words
The way it happens out of nowhere
And all your lines of protection become blurred
If you asked me what love is
I would say it is our deepest truth
The conscious connection beneath our identities
But I warn you, love's meaning has become misused
If you asked me what love is
I could only point you toward what it is not
Lost beneath projections and old fears
As kids we knew love but forgot
If you asked me what love is
I would say with each person I find my answer change
Its meaning evolves as we do
And has a magic that cannot be explained
If you asked me what love is
I would hold up to you a mirror
As you looked into your own eyes
You would find it has always been right here

Miracles

When people ask if you're in love
I hope your answer is always yes
And I do not mean with a person
I hope you fall in love with life a little more each day
For the simple miracle that you woke up that morning
The sun rose again on this planet
And you somehow get to experience a human life

What Meaning Are You Creating?

Every experience that happens to us
Is simply an experience
It is the meaning we create from the experience
That stays with us for a lifetime

The Writer's Curse

Some days I avoid my own pen
Is there anything I can write that has not been said?
These words are my way of making sense of
    a nonsensical world
If I am not writing then I am thinking
And this moment is far too miraculous
To spend lost in the world of my mind
Though I suppose it forces me
To create a life worth writing about

Every Relationship Is a Mirror

You will never accept a love
That is less than the love you have met within yourself

Healing Demands Patience

There are some bruises you cannot see
They run deeper than the surface of the skin
They heal a little with each heartbeat
Be patient as you mend your wounds
Your healing will happen in its own time
—A rose is not constantly blooming

Live in a State of Wonder

Live in a state of wonder. You'll be far more joyful for it, I promise. Wonder is not a forced happiness. Wonder is a passionate curiosity about life. It is a way to make your soul grow. Most of us tread along repeating the same patterns, taking miracles for granted as though they are mere conveniences. We are as honest with ourselves and each other as we can bear, until some challenge happens where we are smacked out of autopilot and forced to become more. How tragic would it be to live your entire life and realize you weren't truly present for any of it? The antidote for overstimulation is wonder. Get outside. Marvel at the stars every once in a while. Hell, even marvel at your phone. That was once just an idea someone had. Who were they? What was their story? Everyone has a story worth telling. Children understand this. They're curious about the world because they're new to it. They aren't waiting to cross an invisible finish line of accomplishment to feel a sense of purpose. They're just in wonder.

You Are Never Alone

What is the difference between us, you ask?
We are separate waves within a vast sea
You have never been alone for a single second
How could you forget we are connected through
   the entire ocean?

Promises

Whisper in my ear
The promise of tomorrow
For a moment it sounds beautiful
But I know that promise to be hollow

Potential

My potential haunts me
As I feel the ghost of who I could be
But I am tired of fantasizing about my future self
Instead of learning to fall in love with who I am right now
Where is the line between self-improvement and
    self-deprecation?

Paint Your Vision

Can you see it? That life you have always wanted within reach of your fingertips. Can you smell the scent of your best friend or lover as they wrap their proud arms around you because you've done it? Can you feel the butterfly in your chest and the tingling in your palms as your whole body comes alive in celebration? Can you hear the laughter of your favorite people as you joke about how scared you were that your dreams wouldn't happen? You have to see it, my love. Every detail of it. It's okay to be scared; that means this is important to you. See it anyway. Paint your vision with all your senses until it comes alive. Until you feel it in your muscles. Until you live your way into it coming true.

Guidance

Go inside and check in with your compass
Allow it to point and follow wherever it leads you
There are no wrong turns
Everyone else will have a million different answers for you
But their opinions will only drown out the whisper of what
   you already know to be true
No amount of outside approval can validate your
   inner knowing
(Trust yourself)

Blank Canvas

Let me become a blank canvas for life to paint on
Let me become a pen for the universe to write with
Let me become the sand the Sun warms with her rays
Let me become the spark that ignites love's flame
I am here to surrender, listening
That is the art of being human
To take part in life unfolding upon itself

The Danger of Comparison

After many rotations around the Earth,
the Sun grew lonely, always watching over everyone
She wanted to be a mountain, strong and unyielding
She wanted to be the sea, wild and uncontainable
She wanted to be a bird, free and able to explore
Her light began to dim as she thought of all the things she
    would rather be than herself
Without her light, the life of the Earth began to wilt
She had forgotten her worth
It was only as she saw
those mountains crumble,
the sea begin to still,
and the birds stop flying,
that she remembered nothing would be the same if she did
    not exist
And so she erupted in flames again, breathing life back into
    the planet she loved so fiercely
All of the creatures on Earth marveled at her radiance
Her light was shining brighter than ever before
She finally understood that
where there is life,
there is love,
and her warmth was the thread that connected it all

5AM

We slipped in and out of each other
Through endless conversations
And what we could not find the words for
Our tender kisses said perfectly

Courage

She learned the most honest thing she could do was to live her life as an endless question—curious, listening, and willing to take the risk of walking into the unknown. When she made a choice, she gave her heart fully to it, because life is not meant to be lived with one foot out the door. She learned that courage was not a test of grandeur but a vulnerable heart willing to embrace each and every life experience. That true courage is made up in the smallest of moments. She learned that strength is being daring enough to say "yes" to your own heart, even if that means saying "no" to someone else's. She learned that awareness means being honest with yourself about everything without shaming yourself for it. Your patterns, desires, attachments, dreams, hopes, and feelings. Most of all, she learned that if she could be courageous in the small moments, it would see her through the big ones.

In or Out

Are you in love with him?
Or are you in love with the way he loves you?

Inspiration

"Where does inspiration come from?" he asked.
She placed her warm hands on his chest and smiled.

My Hope for You

I hope you find freedom
The kind of freedom where the gravity of your
    worries dissolves
and a river of joy runs in your veins
I hope you find purpose
The kind of purpose that doesn't need to be chased
but is discovered within your very breath
I hope you find trust
The kind of trust that embraces every moment
and can find the twinkling star within a blanket
    of darkness
But most of all
I hope you find love
The kind of love that awakens the soul and reminds
    you of your true nature

Give What You Wish to Receive

If you want unconditional love
Learn to give love unconditionally
If you want honesty
Learn to meet the truth inside yourself honestly
If you want true peace
Learn to truly embrace your every piece

Love Is Letting Go

I used to hold on to our moments of bliss
And tuck them away in my heart for safekeeping
Then I realized sometimes love is letting go
Our paths will merge again one day
But for now I smile and think back
To simpler days spent welcoming the morning sun
By kissing its rays on your skin

What Are Your Intentions?

I try but find myself disappointed again
By the shallow intentions of these men
They dream of nights spent skin to skin
But they do not dare touch the heart within
It is far worse when they wear the mask of someone
    who cares
As though I cannot see through that hungry stare
I love myself enough to not seek the validation
Of a man who hides behind the image of vulnerability
When it is really just a presentation

Mother Earth

If you want to know how we are treating our world
Look to how we are treating our women

Borrowed

All that I have lost
Has taught me I never had anything to begin with
Even this body of mine is a borrowed sanctuary
It was when I stopped needing to belong to anything
That I suddenly belonged to everything

Madness

The difference between those who are mad
And those of a sane mind
Is that the sane ones are better at pretending
The artist uses their madness
To fuel the flames of their imagination

Nothing Is Worth Sacrificing Your Joy

I used to ask, "What if?"
I used to ask, "How will I?"
I used to ask, "Is it possible?"
I threw all my worries in a pile
And sparked a match on them
The embers that burned so fiercely
Became the fire from which I danced

Community

Sometimes you meet people, and you immediately get past all the small talk and normal niceties. You find out what puts a sparkle in their eye, what they have been through and the strength it taught them. It takes a certain kind of courage to drop beneath the part of ourselves we're used to presenting. To see and be seen. To feel and be felt. To hear and be heard. This is the double-edged sword of vulnerability—if you avoid it, you avoid the opportunity for lifelong connections. Vulnerability is what we crave most and what we fear most. Everyone has a story that is worth being heard. The key is to be brave enough to tell ours and compassionate enough to listen to theirs.

Woman

She had a madness to her, as wild women often do. She was
a force of nature, you see. Capable of burning what stood
in her way to ash and warming the hearts of those in need
of her glowing embers. When she walked through the dark,
she did not need to look for the light at the end of the
tunnel. She became the light. When she felt fear, she did
not let it snuff out her flames. She used it to spread her
dreams like a forest fire. There were days when she was
a joyful woman. There were days when she was an angry
woman. But no matter the day, she knew every emotion
was beautiful and deserving of her respect. She was a wild
woman, you see. And wild women know the strength it
takes in this world to become free.

Decisions

There has never been a single moment
When you have not held within you the power to change
    your life in an instant
An unlimited number of paths stretch before you
And you may choose any route
Or, with a few simple words, paint an entirely new path . . .
The immeasurable power of decision that belongs to us may
    overwhelm some people
So they stick to the straightest path that appears to be safe
Fearing the blind spots of twists and turns
If only they knew what waited for them just around
    the corner . . .

Questions

Sometimes the answers are in the questions themselves

Who Are You?

"Who are you?" he asked . . .
She began to wander the library of her mind, searching for
an honest answer to his question. Yet all she could find was
what she was not.
"I am not my name.
I am not my body.
I am not my lover.
I am not my art.
I am not my bank account.
I am not my past.
I am not who you think I am.
I am not even who I think I am."
As she continued, panic slowly began to rise inside her as
the many layers of the identity she had crafted over
a lifetime dissolved. In a world where there's an abundance
of knowledge and an absence of wisdom, she felt any
answer slip through her fingertips. "Who are you?" he
asked, smiling this time. As she became more embodied in
the present, she felt herself as consciousness anchored
in absolute neutrality. A simple state of being. Like any
other tree, mountain, river, or form of nature. Yet what
makes being human precious is that we can play in the
world of time. We have all the ingredients to create a recipe
for pleasure or pain.

But the key is to recognize the pieces of our identity as just that . . . ingredients to create our life with as we move through the eternal now.

Unravel the Hurt Inside

I sat with an elder who handed me a string
And told me to tie a knot for every person I have hurt
The first knot I tied was for myself
If that knot did not exist
There would be none after it

Staircases

Imagine if there were a spiraling staircase in your mind, and your life is the journey of walking down to the ground floor. Except on every floor, there is a locked door in your way. And we all have the keys to each other's doors but not our own. So when we encounter the human beings in our life, they can give us a key without even realizing it. But the trick is we have to be present enough to receive the message. We have to learn how to listen for the key. And when we don't, when we focus on the story rather than the lesson, we stay on the same floor. Never deepening further into who we are. But if we go beyond our day-to-day experiences and remember that every single moment was chosen by us so we can find the next key, we won't become trapped in stagnation. And eventually we'll become so integrated in the wisdom of our own being that we'll remember who we are. We'll find the ground floor and reflect back, going, "Ah yes, I see why that had to happen. That was my golden key."

Self-Worth

Self-worth is a funny thing
Most days it's like trying to see myself
Through a funhouse mirror
And believing my warped reflection
Is the person standing here
I'm waiting for the day my perception becomes clear
But reality is a trick of the senses
That my mind tries to define
When reality is undefinable
And looks different through every eye
I watch my heart try to protect itself with pretty walls
But true beauty is what happens
When they finally crumble and fall
Am I truly honest with myself?
Or has vulnerability become another slogan to hide behind
Instead of my feelings honestly being felt?
My sorrow and joy exist on the same line
But I can't walk that line
If from myself I try and hide

Beauty

Beauty is in the details of a person. Those little quirks that may not be obvious on the surface until you make someone feel safe enough to be themselves. It is their imperfections that are often the most interesting. Beauty lives in the smallest of moments, like the warmth of two hearts pressed together, and the sound of a deep breath. Beauty is in the truth that, once someone is a part of your heart, they will be forever. Even if "I love you" becomes "I have to leave you now." Life is long and love is messy, but you will forever occupy a chapter of their story. Beauty is hidden in the most unlikely places, because the most breathtaking things do not demand attention. They quietly invite you to look a little deeper. Whether it's the way the rain feels on your skin or a flower smells blooming in the rocky desert, you can open your heart by falling in love with the beauty of this world again and again.

Care

Speak to me of what you care for
Of what you would bow your heart to
Speak to me of what will matter
When you reflect on all you have been through
Speak to me of your sorrow
And how it has carved your strength
Speak to me of what you love so much
You would fight for at any length

This Is Your Chance

This is the one and only time you will ever exist. This is the one and only time the world will have a chance to know you. This is the one and only time you will be able to love, explore, learn, fail, succeed, and everything in between. Here you are, floating in timeless space. It's all just an experience. I hope you're brave in painting your own path. I hope you don't waste a second of this life covering up who you are or chasing what is not for you. I hope you get a glimpse of just how powerful you are. No one like you has ever existed or will ever exist again. I'll say it again: no one like you has ever existed or will ever exist again.

Acknowledgments

For the reader . . . thank you for going on this journey with me. This book has my heart scattered throughout the pages. I hope you found pieces of yourself within them. I hope you feel understood, supported, and loved. I hope you remember you will always bloom, even within the darkness. And that, whether it is clear to you or not, your path is wherever you step. So step where your heart guides you. Even if we haven't met, I will always care deeply about you.

For my family . . . thank you to my father, who teaches me the strength it takes to be soft. To my mother, who shows me the true meaning of courage. To Alexis, who shows me the medicine of laughter and loyalty.

For my friends . . . thank you for holding my heart, even when it was breaking. For reminding me of the power of an honest word as you listened to every poem, as you were there for every lesson. My life is far more joyful with your bright souls in it.

For my teachers . . . the ones who have passed down their wisdom and smacked me awake when needed. Thank you for making this world a better place and for believing in my growth.

About the Author

Allie Michelle is a bestselling writer, artist, and wellness teacher. Her passion for poetry and storytelling began at a young age, drawing her to language as a way to understand her experience of the world. Her passion for health and wellness has largely influenced her writing. Since the age of seventeen, she has been teaching yoga and meditation and leading transformative retreats around the world. Her first book, *Explorations of a Cosmic Soul*, became an instant Amazon bestseller as a breakout voice in the modern age of poetry. Allie continues to give voice to and touch the hearts of a new generation of poets and artists online, leading a community of dreamers over half a million strong.

Index

Enjoy *The Rose That Blooms in the Night* as an audiobook narrated by the author, wherever audiobooks are sold.